Hot-Air Balloons

Written by Hannah Reed
Photography by Michael Curtain

sundance™

2

Introduction

Hot-air balloons are large flying machines that lift people off the ground.

People have been flying in hot-air balloons for more than two hundred years. The first hot-air balloon flight was in France, in 1783.

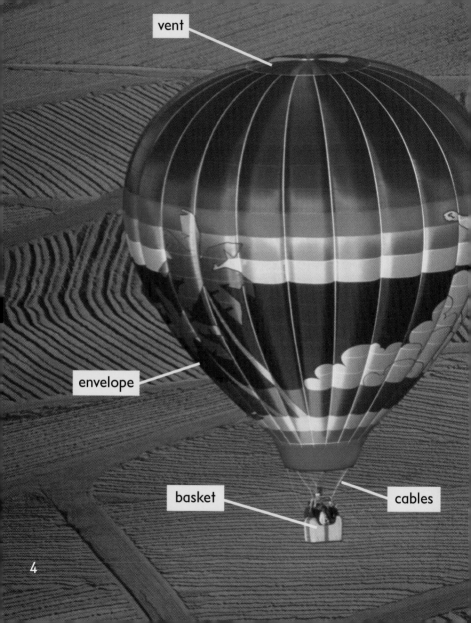

vent

envelope

basket

cables

How a Hot-Air Balloon Flies

Hot-air balloons can fly because the hot air inside the balloon is lighter than the cold air outside.

A hot-air balloon has a basket, a burner, and a balloon called an envelope. As the hot air rises, it lifts the envelope and basket off the ground. To keep flying, the air inside the envelope must stay hot. The burner heats the air.

The basket carries the pilot and the passengers, as well as the flight instruments, the burner, and the fuel cylinders.

5

burner

Setting Up

Hot-air balloons don't take up much space until they are blown up.

The envelope is very heavy. It can weigh more than 154 pounds (70 kilograms).

The envelope, the basket, and the burner are driven in a truck to the take-off field. A team of people unload the balloon and get it ready to fly.

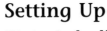

Filling the Envelope

Before the hot-air balloon can fly, the envelope must be filled with hot air. The envelope is unfolded and joined to the basket, which is laid on its side.

The burner is then lit to blow hot air into the envelope.

People hold the bottom of the envelope open. When there is enough hot air inside the envelope, it stays open by itself.

9

10

Taking Off

As the envelope fills with hot air, it begins to rise until it is upright. While it is filling, it must be tied to the ground to keep it from flying away.

When the pilot and the passengers are in the basket, the hot-air balloon takes off.

In the Air

Hot-air balloons go where the wind pushes them. Pilots take the balloons to different heights to look for winds blowing in the direction they want to go.

People on the ground follow hot-air balloons in cars and trucks. These people are called the chase crew. They talk to the pilot on a two-way radio. When the pilot is ready, the chase crew helps to land the balloon.

Balloonists do not usually fly at night. Balloons might get caught in power lines. It is also difficult to find a place to land.

14

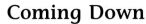

Coming Down

To land the hot-air balloon, the air inside the envelope needs to cool. The pilot turns down the burner and opens a vent in the top of the envelope.

As hot air escapes through the vent, cool air is sucked in through the bottom of the envelope. The cool air makes the balloon heavier, and it starts to lose height.

The pilot can control how quickly the air inside the envelope cools down. He does this by turning the burner up and down and by opening and closing the vent.

Hot-air balloons are used in many ways. Some are used to collect scientific facts. Others are used for advertising. Many are used for sight-seeing and for the fun of flying.